HAL•LEONARD INSTRUMENTAL PLAY-ALONG

AUDIO ACCESS INCLUDED

PLAYBACK+
Speed • Pitch • Balance • Loop

CLARINET

Disney FROZEN II

T0087304

Audio arrangements by Peter Deneff

To access audio visit:
www.halleonard.com/mylibrary

Enter Code
6554-3985-1291-0014

Disney Characters and Artwork © 2019 Disney

ISBN 978-1-5400-8375-3

HAL•LEONARD®

Visit Hal Leonard Online at
www.halleonard.com

Contact us:
Hal Leonard
7777 West Bluemound Road
Milwaukee, WI 53213
Email: info@halleonard.com

In Europe, contact:
Hal Leonard Europe Limited
42 Wigmore Street
Marylebone, London, W1U 2RN
Email: info@halleonardeurope.com

In Australia, contact:
Hal Leonard Australia Pty. Ltd.
4 Lentara Court
Cheltenham, Victoria, 3192 Australia
Email: info@halleonard.com.au

ALL IS FOUND

Clarinet

Music and Lyrics by KRISTEN ANDERSON-LOPEZ
and ROBERT LOPEZ

SOME THINGS NEVER CHANGE

Clarinet

Music and Lyrics by KRISTEN ANDERSON-LOPEZ
and ROBERT LOPEZ

INTO THE UNKNOWN

Clarinet

Music and Lyrics by KRISTEN ANDERSON-LOPEZ
and ROBERT LOPEZ

LOST IN THE WOODS

CLARINET

Music and Lyrics by KRISTEN ANDERSON-LOPEZ
and ROBERT LOPEZ

THE NEXT RIGHT THING

CLARINET

Music and Lyrics by KRISTEN ANDERSON-LOPEZ
and ROBERT LOPEZ

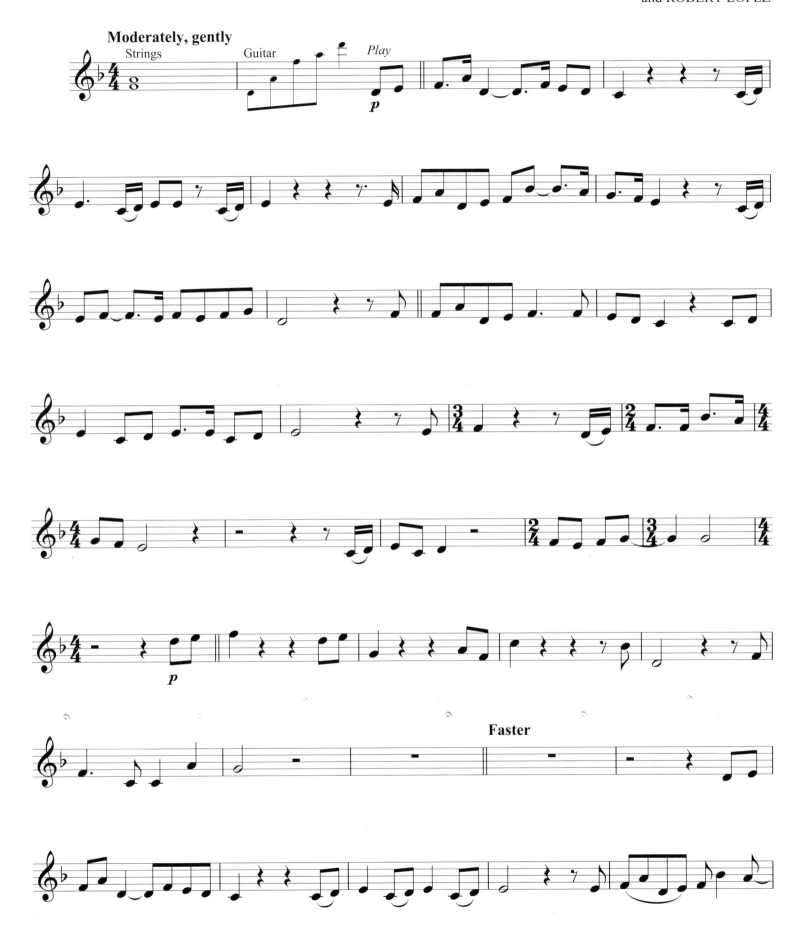

REINDEER(S) ARE BETTER THAN PEOPLE (CONT.)

CLARINET

Music and Lyrics by KRISTEN ANDERSON-LOPEZ
and ROBERT LOPEZ

SHOW YOURSELF

WHEN I AM OLDER

Clarinet

Music and Lyrics by KRISTEN ANDERSON-LOPEZ
and ROBERT LOPEZ